W9-BGO-945

SUPER SAVING
TAX SECRETS

SUPER SAVING
TAX SECRETS

BY JEANNE BOSSOLINA LUBIN
AND
BRUCE LUBIN

Castle Point
Publishing
Hoboken, NJ

Printed in China

Cover and Interior design by Quadrum Solutions Pvt. Ltd.
ISBN 978-0-9820667-4-4

PLEASE NOTE: While we've made every effort to provide useful and accurate information in this book, we cannot guarantee that the information is correct or appropriate for your particular situation. Tax laws and regulations change often and are subject to different interpretations. It is your responsibility to verify all information and all laws discussed in this book before relying on them, and you should always seek the advice of a tax professional.

DEDICATION

To Clack, Moose, and Stink, as always

ACKNOWLEDGMENTS

Thanks to Joy Mangano, Brian Scevola, Karen Matsu Greenberg, Jennifer Boudinot, and the team at Quadrum Solutions. Extra-special thanks to Bob Lubin, without whose expertise this book would not be possible.

CONTENTS

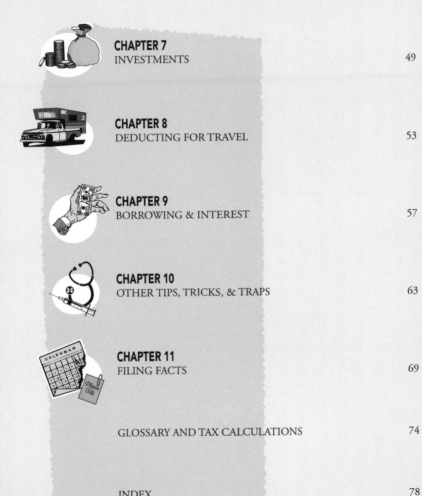

THE BASICS ^{chapter}

1

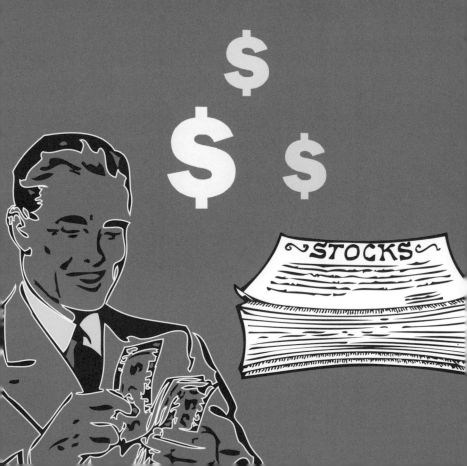

FROM THE IRS

CHOOSING A TAX PREPARER

While most preparers provide honest service to their clients, the IRS urges taxpayers to be careful when choosing a preparer—as careful as they would be choosing a doctor or lawyer. Even if someone else prepares a tax return, the taxpayer is ultimately responsible for all the information on the return. For that reason, taxpayers should never sign a blank tax form, and they should always review the return before signing it and ask questions on entries they don't understand. Here are more helpful hints from the IRS for choosing a tax return preparer.

1.   Be cautious of tax preparers who claim they can obtain larger refunds than other preparers.

2.   Avoid preparers who base their fee on a percentage of the refund.

3.   Use a reputable tax professional who signs the tax return and provides a copy.

4.   Consider whether the individual or firm will be around to answer questions about the preparation of the tax return months, or even years, after the return has been filed.

5.   Check the person's credentials. Only attorneys, certified public accountants (CPAs) and enrolled agents can represent taxpayers before the IRS in all matters, including audits, collection and appeals. Other return preparers may only represent taxpayers for audits of returns they actually prepared.

6.   Find out if the preparer is affiliated with a professional organization that provides its members with continuing education and resources and holds them to a code of ethics.

7.   Ask friends and family whether they know anyone who has used the tax professional and whether they were satisfied with the service they received.

WHO KNEW?

Tax evasion is serious business! Remember Richard Hatch, the winner of the first season of *Survivor*? He didn't report the $1 million he won on the show, and was sentenced to almost five years in jail.

HOW TO USE THIS BOOK

Everyone has heard the old saying "nothing is certain but death and taxes." You can't do anything about death, but with a bit of planning you can drastically reduce the amount of taxes you pay each year! On the following pages, we'll provide you with straightforward solutions to save you money with simple-to-understand (but frequently overlooked) strategies and tips for your taxes. These techniques—organized by subject matter so you can easily find those at apply to you—will give you strategies that are easy to implement, even if you normally feel like an idiot when it comes time to slog through that maze of IRS schedules and forms. The key is to start early enough that you can evaluate your circumstances and make appropriate planning moves before the end of the year.

WHAT IS TAX PLANNING AND WHY SHOULD I DO IT?

Tax planning means nothing more than taking steps that will minimize the taxes you have to pay each year. Many people don't plan at all, and still others start planning only a few days before April 15—and in both cases they usually wind up paying more than they need to. Just as you compare prices from different stores to save money, you can make different choices about your taxes that will save you money. We're not talking about cheating (known as "tax evasion")—for example, not reporting all your income to the IRS. Tax evasion is illegal, and people who get caught doing it not only must pay all the taxes they owe, plus interest and penalties, but they may even go to jail. Tax planning, however, is legal, ethical, and makes sense for everyone who has to pay taxes.

ALL THOSE PUBLICATIONS...

Throughout this book you'll find instructions pointing you to particular IRS publications that will give you more information about the topic at hand. To obtain them, call 1-800-TAX-FORM (1-800-829-3676), ask at your local library, or visit IRS.gov and type "publication 501" (for example) in the search box at the top of the page.

WHO KNEW?

The biggest mistake people make on their tax returns is taking the standard deduction when they should be itemizing. Government statistics show that over 2 million taxpayers overpay their taxes by an average of $610 because they fail to itemize.

BACK TO SCHOOL

The start of the school year is a good time to start making a simple projection of how much you'll owe in taxes before you implement any tax-planning steps. Estimate your income and expenses for the year based on how much you've earned and spent so far. You can do this fairly easily with tax preparation software such as TurboTax. There are also several websites that have online tax calculators (H&R Block and Taxbrain.com are good examples), but they don't have as much information as the software packages. When you come up with a projected tax bill, consider it a starting point. As you go through this book and see which tips you can use, you can plug in the numbers into your projection and see how much you can save.

THE STATE OF IT

This book covers only federal income taxes (those that are paid to the IRS), but forty-three states also impose their own income taxes. Most of them use the same information and guidelines as the federal taxes, so using the tips in this book will probably lower your state taxes as well. For more information on your state income taxes, the best place to start is the website of your state's tax department. A useful directory of these websites is available at Taxsites.com/state.html.

WHAT THEY ARE: ITEMIZING VS. THE STANDARD DEDUCTION

The standard deduction is just what it sounds like—a flat amount that you can deduct from your taxable income. The amount you can deduct is based on your filing status (married or single), number of dependents, and what year you're filing taxes for. For additional information on the standard deduction, see IRS Publication 501. When you itemize deductions, you have the ability to deduct the actual dollar amount of certain expenses. Expenses that you can list on your itemized deductions include mortgage interest, property taxes, medical expenses, and more. If you total up all of your allowable deductions and the sum is greater than the standard deduction, it's wise to itemize!

WHAT EXPENSES CAN BE ITEMIZED?

To find out about all of the expenses that can be deducted when itemizing your deductions, check out the instructions for Schedule A of your 1040. The most common expenses include:
- Mortgage interest
- Charitable contributions
- Property taxes
- State and local income taxes
- Medical expenses that exceed 7.5 percent of your adjusted gross income
- Certain miscellaneous expenses that exceed 2 percent of your income, such as union dues, tools and supplies needed for your job, tax preparation fees, some legal fees, and many more

SHOULD YOU ITEMIZE?

If your itemized deductions are greater than your standard deduction, then the answer is YES. To determine if itemizing would be worthwhile, you should take a look at Schedule A of Form 1040. On this sheet, you can list your itemized expenses and then total them up to compare the amount to the standard deduction. If the itemized amount is greater, then you want to itemize. If the total itemized amount is less than the standard deduction, you don't want to itemize. The largest deductions for most people come in

TO ITEMIZE OR NOT TO ITEMIZE...

...that is the question—and the wrong answer could cost you plenty! When it comes to reducing your tax bill, itemizing deductions is often the way to go, especially if you're a homeowner. While taking the standard deduction is easier (and might be a better option if you have a simple tax situation or rent your home), itemizing your deductions could lead to substantial savings.

the form of mortgage interest and property taxes. With these deductions, even a modest mortgage could put you over the standard deduction. And since mortgage interest and property taxes are often thousands of dollars more than the standard deduction, the tax savings can be significant.

IF YOU CAN'T PROVE IT, YOU WON'T GET IT

When tax time comes around, do you dig frantically through piles of papers looking for the documentation you need to prepare your tax returns? Are you unsure about which records you should keep and which ones you can safely throw away? Make your life easier and ensure that you don't miss any deductions by organizing your record keeping system early in the year and keeping it up-to-date. Not only does having organized records make it easier (and less frustrating) for you to file your tax return, it also enables you to explain an item on your return that the IRS might question, which could prevent you from having to pay additional taxes and penalties for unsubstantiated items.

NOT ALL THE SHARKS ARE IN THE SEA: TAX ANTICIPATION LOANS

Have you filed your taxes and discovered that you will be receiving a refund? If you're like most people, you probably want to get your hands on that money as soon as possible, but this could be costly. Many tax preparers offer "instant" tax refunds, otherwise known as tax refund anticipation loans, that can give you cash on the spot or within a day or two.

• How refund anticipation loans work. When you file your taxes, it can take a few weeks for the IRS to issue a check or send your direct deposit, so a tax refund anticipation loan is a way

to get your refund without waiting. You aren't just getting your refund early, however: these are short-term loans that are issued by a bank and are secured by your expected refund. Since these are loans, interest and fees do apply. The problem is that the fees are generally not clear, as they are automatically deducted from your refund by the company offering them, and are not presented in terms consumers are familiar with. In some cases, the fees on an anticipation loan are the equivalent of over 200% APR!

• It pays to wait. While it would be nice to get your hard-earned money back in your pocket as quickly as possible, it is to your advantage if you can wait for your refund. If you file electronically and request direct deposit, you should expect your refund in as little as two weeks. Those few weeks could save you a few hundred dollars in fees that you would have otherwise spent on a refund anticipation loan.

• Alternatives to consider. While credit cards shouldn't be a short-term financial fix, it is important to note that even the worst credit card is going to charge you less in interest than the best refund anticipation loan. Ideally, you don't want to use credit cards for this purpose, but it could be an acceptable option. If you consistently rely on the extra money provided by your tax refund, you may want to consider adjusting your withholding on your W-4. With the right exemptions, you can put more money in your pocket every paycheck so that you don't have a big refund just once a year.

BUNDLE UP TO SAVE A BUNDLE

Expenses such as tax preparation fees, safety deposit box fees, and investment fees are deductible only to the extent that they exceed 2 percent of your adjusted gross income. But if you "bundle" two years' worth of investment—and tax prep–related expenses by paying ahead of time, you can maximize your itemized tax deductions. For example, if your AGI is $50,000 a year, then you can only deduct any expenses that are over $1,000 (2 percent of $50,000). If you have out-of-pocket expenses related to investments and tax preparation that total $1,500, only $500 would be eligible to be listed as an itemized tax deduction. If you work with advisors you trust, you may consider pre-paying for tax preparation and investment advisory/financial planning services for the following year. In this way, two years of expenses can be bundled into a single calendar year and more of it will be deductible.

CREDITS VS. DEDUCTIONS

Throughout this book we discuss tax credits and tax deductions. What's the difference? A deduction reduces your taxable income, while a credit reduces your tax bill. In other words, a deduction lowers the amount of income you've made, making your tax less. But a credit doesn't reduce your income—it's subtracted directly from the amount of taxes you owe. Since they're basically like free money from the government, credits are much better than deductions. For example, if you are in the bracket that must pay 33 percent of your income, a $1,000 deduction would only reduce the amount of your taxable income, saving you $333 in taxes. On the other hand, a $1,000 tax credit simply saves you $1,000 in taxes. (You'd need a tax deduction of $3,000 to give you the same benefit as a tax credit of $1,000!)

WHAT RECORDS YOU SHOULD KEEP

• Your checkbook can help you remember income and expenses that should be reported on your tax return, but the checkbook and cancelled checks alone aren't sufficient documentation to prove the deductibility of an expense.

• In addition to proof of payment (such as cancelled checks and credit card receipts), you also need invoices, receipts, sales slips, or other written documentation that spells out exactly what you paid for.

• Deductions that you need to document include alimony, charitable contributions, mortgage interest, child care expenses, and real estate taxes. If you make payments in cash, get a signed and dated receipt showing the amount and a description.

• To prove that you correctly claimed income from investments such as stocks, bonds, and mutual funds, you need to be able to determine your basis and whether you have a gain or loss when you sold them. Your records should show the purchase price, sales price, commissions, dividends received in cash or reinvested, stock splits, load charges, and original issue discount (OID). An Excel spreadsheet is a great way to track this information, but even a handwritten schedule will do.

• If you have deductible expenses withheld from your paycheck, such as union dues, medical insurance premiums, or 401(k) contributions, keep your pay stubs as proof of payment.

• Specific records you should keep also include: copies of W-2 and 1099 forms, bank statements, brokerage and mutual fund statements, Form K-1 (for partnerships), sales slips, invoices, credit card receipts, sales agreements, closing statements, and insurance records.

HOW LONG DO I KEEP THIS STUFF?

Although legally you need only keep tax records for three years from the date you filed the related income tax return, you should keep a copy of your actual tax returns, W-2s, 1099s, and any other tax forms indefinitely. The IRS destroys original tax returns after three years, and you or your heirs may need information from the returns at some point, or you may need to prove your earnings for Social Security purposes.

NOTES

YOU & YOUR FAMILY

chapter 2

THE SHIFT KEY

Tax rates in the U.S. range from 10 to 35 percent, with many brackets in between. One time-honored method of saving tax dollars is to shift your income from a higher bracket to someone in a lower bracket—namely, your child. Income shifting works best for people in high tax brackets, especially if they own their own business or have assets that have appreciated in value. Recent tax law changes (like the "kiddie tax") have made it more difficult, but it's still possible. However, the IRS does not allow you to just allocate part of your salary to your children and have them pay tax on it. The easiest ways to utilize income shifting are:

• Transferring ownership of income-producing assets to your children, grandchildren, or others in a lower tax bracket, or

• Hiring your children or other relatives to work for your business and pay them a salary.

SHIFTY IS THRIFTY

Shifting income provides benefits in addition to just the lower tax rate on the income. It also achieves the following:

• By reducing your adjusted gross income (AGI), you reverse the process by which many exemptions, deductions, and credits are phased out as your AGI goes up. Some deductions are available only to the extent that they exceed a specific percentage of your AGI. (For example, only the portion of medical expenses that exceed 7.5 percent of your AGI are deductible.) The lower your AGI, the more deductions and credits you get to keep.

• Giving away assets reduces the size of your estate when you die. While you never know what the tax rate on estates will be when it's your time to go, it is safe to say that the smaller your estate, the smaller your estate taxes.

THANKS, GRANDMA!

Parents, grandparents, and other relatives love to give children things like stocks, bonds, and mutual funds. These assets generate investment income in the form of interest, dividends, and profits from sales. This is called "unearned income" because the owner didn't actually have to work at a job to make the money. While your child doesn't have to pay tax for receiving the gift, he or she will be responsible for paying tax on the unearned income it generates. How this is taxed depends on the child's age. Children under nineteen don't have to pay tax on their first $900 of income each year, since that's the amount of their minimum standard deduction. Therefore, giving children income-producing investments a great way of creating a modest amount of tax-free income.

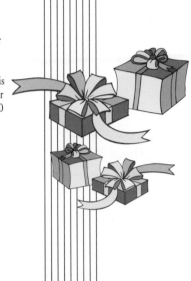

INHERITANCE

When you inherit an asset (such as real estate, stock, or mutual funds), your cost basis is the fair market value at the date the person died. It doesn't matter that the deceased bought the asset at a lower cost. As a result of this "stepped

BE CAREFUL!

Before giving assets to your kids, make sure you consider the potential drawbacks, and don't forget that you must first give up ownership of the assets! Even if you set up a custodial account (like a UGMA or UTMA), you can control the funds as custodian only until the children reach age eighteen or twenty-one (depending on the state). After that, they can use the funds for anything they want, whether it's college or a new motorcycle.

up" basis rule, when the person died, he or she escaped the tax on the difference between the original cost and the market value at death—and you'll escape the tax, too. It's a good idea to keep a record of the market value on the date of death. That's easy for a security, but you may want to get an appraisal for an asset that is harder to value, like real estate.

DOCTOR, DOCTOR, GIVE ME THE NEWS

You certainly don't need a book to tell you that medical care for most Americans is very expensive. Even those with insurance pay out of pocket for things like co-payments, non-covered procedures, and sometimes even a portion of the premiums. Taxpayers who itemize can deduct medical and dental expenses for themselves, their spouses, and their dependents. Eligible expenses include both the out-of-pocket expenses not covered or reimbursed by your insurance, and the premiums themselves. The bad news is that you can only deduct the amount of these expenses that exceeds 7.5 percent of your adjusted gross income (AGI). This hefty limitation on the deduction makes it useless for many taxpayers, but if you've had surgery or lots of medical procedures this year, you probably qualify. An example: Let's say your AGI is $50,000 a year. This means that your medical costs have to be higher than 7.5 percent of $50,000, or $3,750. So if you have out-of-pocket medical expenses of $4,000, only $250 (the amount that exceeds $3,750) would be eligible as an itemized tax deduction.

HOW ABOUT ANOTHER KID?

People who adopt a child are entitled to a tax credit of 100 percent of their adoption expenses up to $12,150 (in 2009). Be aware that this credit phases out for taxpayers with higher income, and is reduced to zero for taxpayers with AGI over $222,180.

YOUR HOME & CAR

chapter 3

FROM THE IRS

TIPS FOR DEDUCTING DAMAGE TO YOUR HOME OR CAR

Taxpayers who find themselves the victim of a natural disaster or theft should know the rules for deducting their casualty losses next year when they file their federal tax return. Generally, you may deduct losses to your home, household items, and vehicles on your federal income tax return. Here are ten things the IRS wants you to know about deducting casualty or theft losses. For more information, see Publication 547: Casualties, Disasters, and Thefts.

1.   A casualty loss can result from the damage, destruction, or loss of your property from any sudden, unexpected, and unusual event such as a flood, hurricane, tornado, fire, earthquake, or even volcanic eruption.

2.   If your property is not completely destroyed, or if it is personal-use property, the amount of your casualty or theft loss is the lesser of: the adjusted basis of your property, or the decrease in fair market value of your property as a result of the casualty or theft. The adjusted basis of your property is usually your cost, increased or decreased by certain events such as improvements or depreciation. You may determine the decrease in fair market value by appraisal or, if certain conditions are met, by the cost of repairing the property. Keep in mind the general definition of fair market value is the price at which property would change hands between a buyer and seller, neither having to buy or sell, and both having reasonable knowledge of all necessary facts.

WHO KNEW?

What's one of the biggest tax myths? According to a survey by CCH, three out of ten taxpayers wrongly believe that they can write off losses from a home sale.

3. If the property was held by you for personal use, you must further reduce your loss by $100. This $100 reduction for losses of personal-use property applies to each casualty or theft event that occurred during the year. However, for 2009, this reduction has increased to $500. The total of all your casualty and theft losses of personal-use property must be further reduced by 10 percent of your adjusted gross income.

4. Recent legislation changed some of the tax rules pertaining to losses resulting from federally declared disasters. The new law removes the 10 percent of adjusted gross income limitation for net disaster losses and allows individuals to claim the net disaster losses even if they do not itemize their deductions. The new law is effective for disasters 2008 and 2009.

5. If your business or income-producing property is completely destroyed, the decrease in fair market value is not considered. Your loss is the adjusted basis of the property, minus any salvage value and any insurance or other reimbursement you receive or expect to receive. For more information on determining adjusted basis, see Publication 551: Basis of Assets.

6. In figuring your loss, do not consider the loss of future profits or income due to the casualty.

7. Casualty losses are generally deductible only in the year the casualty occurred. However, if you have a deductible loss from a disaster in a federally declared disaster area, you can choose to deduct that loss on your tax return for the year immediately preceding the year of the casualty. Generally, you must make the choice to use the preceding year by the due date of the current year's return, without extensions.

SHOULD I STAY?

The single most effective way to avoid capital gains taxes on your property is, of course, to make it your permanent home. There's even a second tax bonus to staying put—when you die, your home's value for tax purposes is "stepped up" to its fair market value. This means that no tax would ever have to be paid, by you or your heirs, on the appreciation your home earned while you were alive.

LET UNCLE SAM HELP BUY YOUR FIRST HOUSE

A tax credit of up to $8,000 is available for first-time home buyers who purchased a primary residence after January 1, 2009 and before December 1, 2009. A first time buyer is defined as one who has not owned a residence in the US during the prior three years, so if that's you, make sure you take this credit! Just be aware that there is an income limit—if you make $75,000 (for single returns) or $150,000 (for joint returns) the credit is less, and eliminated completely if you make more than $95,000 (single) or $170,000 (joint).

GO GREEN AND GET MONEY!

If you made an energy-efficient improvement on your existing home, you may be eligible for a tax credit! The credit is for 30 percent of the cost of the improvement, and is available through 2016 on the following items:

• Geothermal heat pumps
• Solar panels
• Solar water heaters
• Small wind energy systems
• Fuel cells

The credit is also available for these items, but only up to $1,500, and only through 2010:

• Insulation
• Metal and asphalt roofs
• Heating, ventilation, and air conditioning systems
• Water heaters (non-solar)
• Biomass stoves

For more info, go to Energystar.gov and click on "Tax credits for energy efficiency."

MAKE THE BEST OF YOUR MORTGAGE REFI

If your home is in foreclosure or you've if worked out a plan with your lender to reduce your mortgage debt, there's an extra tax benefit that accompanies getting your debt reduced. Usually, canceled debt is counted as income. But under a new rule, the IRS will let you exempt that charge on up to $2 million (for joint returns) or $1 million (for single returns). Example: You borrow $10,000 and default on the loan after paying back $2,000. If the lender is unable to collect the remaining debt from you, there is a cancellation of debt of $8,000, which is usually taxable income to you. But this exemption eliminates that extra tax, although it's important to remember the exemption only counts on primary residences, so speculators are out of luck. For more from the IRS on the Mortgage Forgiveness Debt Relief Act of 2007 look for their Publication 4681: Canceled Debts, Foreclosures, Repossessions, and Abandonments.

DEDUCT THE SALES TAX, JACK

The IRS announced that taxpayers who purchase a new passenger vehicle in 2009 may be entitled to deduct both state and local sales and excise taxes paid on their 2009 tax returns. This tax break is only available for 2009 tax returns and could amount to $300 off the price of a typically priced new car. On its own, that's not enough to persuade most people to buy a new car, but if you're already planning to hit the showrooms, it might help. Combined with the incentives currently offered by many dealers for rebates and low interest rates, 2009 was a very good time to purchase a new car. By utilizing this deduction you will get cash back on your tax return, kind of like a delayed rebate. The deduction is limited to the state and local sales and excise taxes paid on up to $49,500 of the purchase price of a qualified new car, light truck, motor home, or motorcycle. The amount of the deduction can be phased out. If your adjusted gross income is between $125,000 and $135,000 as an individual filers or between $250,000 and $260,000 for joint filers, the deduction can be phased out. The vehicle must be purchased after February 6, 2009, and before January 1, 2010, in order to qualify for the deduction. You may utilize this deduction even if you don't itemize on your return.

TAX-FREE HOUSE RENTAL

Did you know that homeowners are allowed to rent out their homes for up to fourteen days without paying a cent on the rental income? As long as it is a home that you use for at least fifteen days a year, it doesn't matter if it's a vacation home, a second home, or your principal residence—it's tax-free money. You don't have to file Schedule E as landlords do, but you also don't get to deduct operating expenses or depreciation for the (tiny) rental period. However, you can still deduct your home mortgage interest and real estate taxes just like every other homeowner.

OR SHOULD I GO?

We wouldn't suggest selling your home just to get a tax break, but if you are planning on selling, you may qualify for the biggest tax break you'll ever get. If you meet certain requirements, you won't have to pay any tax on up to $250,000 of the gain from the sale of your principal home if you're single, or up to $500,000 if you're married and file jointly. Even if your local market is flat right now, US real estate prices have historically moved steadily upward through the years. So the time will probably come when you'll be able to take advantage of the exclusion. Here's what you need to know.

• Obviously, this tax break doesn't do you much good if you're in a bad housing market and you sell your house for less than you paid for it. To add insult to injury, you can't write off losses on a home sale! If possible, try to wait until the housing market goes back up.

• Timing is everything! The most important thing you need to know to qualify for the $250,000/$500,000 exclusion is that you must own and occupy the home as your principal residence for at least two years before you sell it. However, you don't have to be living in the home when you sell it—your two years of occupation can occur anytime during the five years before you sell. Also, the years of ownership and years of occupying don't need to overlap! As long as you have two years of ownership and two years of use during the five years before selling, you're okay. This is important for renters who end up purchasing their rental properties. The time they lived in the home as tenants counts as "use," even though they didn't own it at the time.

• This exclusion can seem like the gift that keeps on giving, because you can do anything you want with the tax-free proceeds from the sale. Best of

WHO KNEW?

As of July 1, 2009, the deduction allowed for driving a car for business increased to 58.5 cents (from 50.5). The deduction for driving as a medical or moving expense also went up, to 27 cents from 19 cents

all, if you buy another home, you can qualify for the exclusion in another two years, and you can use this exclusion any number of times over your lifetime as long as you satisfy the requirements. By wisely using this generous exclusion, you can buy and sell many homes over the years and avoid income taxes on all or some of your profits.

• Unfortunately, if you don't qualify, or if your profit is more than the exclusion amount, you'll have to pay tax on the gain. If you owned the house for at least one year, you'll qualify for long-term capital gains tax rate, which is currently 15 percent for most taxpayers. And if you owned the home for less than one year the gain will be taxed at your ordinary income tax rate, just like your salary.

VERY INTEREST-ING

Taxpayers can claim a deduction on interest paid on a loan secured by their first or second home. Most home equity loans fall into this category, but it's easy to get confused if you have multiple "second" homes or mortgages in excess of a home's value. For details on if your home qualifies, see IRS Publication 936, Section 1. This goes without saying, but the benefit of deducting mortgage interest is that you save money. For example, you may use a home equity loan as part of a debt consolidation program. Suddenly, the interest you pay becomes tax deductible—not just an expense. Of course, you still have to make the debt go away, but if you run the numbers this can work out in your favor.

YOUR NEW, GREEN CAR

If you've had enough of high gas prices, Congress wants to give you a nudge to consider a hybrid vehicle. Hybrids, like the popular Toyota Prius, are powered by both an internal combustion

WE ALL HAVE OUR LIMITS

If you think you may qualify for interest deduction from your home equity loan, it's important to know that it is not unlimited. You can generally deduct interest you pay on the first $100,000 of a home equity loan. After that, it depends. If the home equity loan was used to improve your first or second home—or to purchase a second home—you can probably take the deduction on an amount up to $1 million or the value of the home. IRS Publication 936 Section 2 contains more detail. If you use the alternative minimum tax (AMT) on your 1040, your home equity loan deductions will only help you if you used the money for home improvements.

engine and a rechargeable battery, and can get mileage of over 65 miles per gallon. While they are more expensive, a new hybrid vehicle tax credit was enacted to encourage people to buy these cars and reduce our nation's dependence on foreign oil. Almost anyone who purchases a new hybrid before December 21, 2010 is eligible for a credit between $3,400 and $12,000. To qualify for the credit, the hybrid must be on the IRS certified list of hybrids (check their website at Irs. gov). This only applies to buying, not leasing, the vehicle.

Figuring the actual amount of the credit is tricky. First, once a manufacturer sells 60,000 vehicles, the credit starts to get phased out over fifteen months for all hybrids by that company. So you must act fast if you've got your eye on a particular model. (Sorry, the Prius is no longer eligible.) Second, the size of the credit is determined by a complex formula based on each vehicle's fuel efficiency. To find out more, visit Fueleconomy.gov/Feg/tax_hybrid.shtml

GOODBYE, OLD PAL

If you have an old car you want to get rid of, donating it to charity can seem like a great idea. It's an easy thing to do and it gives you a charitable deduction. The problem is that many people in recent years had the same idea, and too many of them abused the tax rules by grossly inflating the value of their old junker, sometimes claiming a deduction for thousands on a bomb that the charity ultimately sold for less than $100. So the IRS tightened up these regulations recently. Now, if you donate a car and claim a deduction greater than $500, your deduction is limited to the amount that the charity receives when it actually sells the car. The charity must provide you with an IRS Form 1098-C (Contributions of Motor Vehicles, Boats, and Airplanes), which documents the sale price, and must be attached to your return. To learn more, see IRS Publication 4303: A Donor's Guide to Vehicle Donations.

EDUCATION COSTS

4

FROM THE IRS

DOES THE IRS OWE YOU MONEY?

Who couldn't use a little extra cash? The IRS may have some money for you. Here is what you need to know about claiming money.

1. If you have not filed a prior year tax return and are due a refund, you should consider filing the return to claim that refund. If you are missing a refund for a previously filed tax return, you should contact the IRS to check the status of your refund and confirm your current address.

2. Some people may have had taxes withheld from their wages but were not required to file a tax return because they had too little income. Others may not have had any tax withheld but would be eligible for the refundable earned income tax credit. To collect this money a return must be filed with the IRS no later than three years from the due date of the return.

3. If no return is filed to claim a refund within three years, the money becomes the property of the US Treasury.

4. There is no penalty assessed by the IRS for filing a late return qualifying for a refund.

5. Were you expecting a refund you never received? Refund checks are mailed to your last known address. Checks are returned to the IRS if you move without notifying the IRS or the US Postal Service.

6. You may be able to update your address with the IRS on the "Where's My Refund?" feature available on IRS.gov. You will be prompted to provide an updated address if there is an undeliverable check outstanding within the last 12 months.

TUITION AND FEES DEDUCTION

Up to a maximum of $4,000 per year, you can take a tax deduction for college tuition and other mandatory school fees paid for yourself, your spouse, or your dependent. The deduction is reduced for taxpayers with higher income and disappears entirely if you have an AGI of more than $80,000 (or $160,000 for joint filers). Note that this deduction is temporary—2009 is scheduled to be the last year that it's available.

OFF TO COLLEGE TO GET SOME KNOWLEDGE

Just about everyone agrees on the importance of education—for ourselves, our children, and our grandchildren—but getting there can be expensive. Perhaps thinking that well-educated taxpayers will earn more money and pay more taxes, lawmakers have added multiple tax benefits to help people paying for higher education. Unfortunately, millions of families leave money on the table every year by overlooking the valuable tax breaks available, including:
- Tuition and fees deduction
- The American opportunity credit (formerly known as the hope tax credit)
- The lifetime learning credit

AMERICAN OPPORTUNITY CREDIT

The American opportunity tax credit is a refundable tax credit for undergraduate college education expenses that you can claim if you, your spouse, or your dependent are enrolled at least half-time at an eligible education institution, and you were responsible for paying college expenses. This credit provides up to $2,500 for the first $4,000 of qualifying educational expenses. This credit is scheduled to have a limited life span: it will be available only for the years 2009 and 2010, unless Congress decides to extend the credit to other years.

WHICH CREDIT IS FOR YOU?

You can't take both the American opportunity credit and the lifetime learning credit in the same year for the same person. In addition, these tax credits have different income ranges than the tuition & fees Deduction. The best advice is to

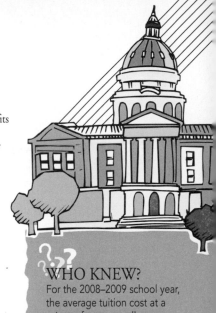

WHO KNEW?
For the 2008–2009 school year, the average tuition cost at a private, four-year college was $25,143. At public universities it was $6,585.

see which tax break you qualify for, and if you qualify for both the deduction and the tax credits, to go with the tax break that provides the largest benefit. To learn more, see IRS Publication 970: Tax Benefits for Education.

CATCH A RIDE ON THE 529

Uncle Sam doesn't normally advise families how to invest their money. But it seems clear that the feds now believe 529 college savings accounts are the best option for most Americans struggling to keep up with rising educational costs. Almost every family with children should now strongly consider putting at least some college savings into a 529 plan. Here's why: First, these state-sponsored investment accounts—offered by nearly all states and the District of Columbia—allow parents and grandparents to invest large sums (often $300,000 or more per beneficiary). Moreover, just as with a 401(k), money invested in a 529 is allowed to grow and compound tax-free! That offers parents a huge advantage over traditional brokerage accounts, whose gains, dividends, and interest income all are taxed along the way. Finally, 529s are advantageous from a financial-aid standpoint, because none of the money held in a 529 is considered the student's asset when calculating aid eligibility. One key provision that made 529s popular—the ability to withdraw money from these accounts tax-free for qualified educational expenses—was to expire in 2010. But the Pension Protection Act of 2006 made withdrawals from 529s permanently tax-free when used for qualified purposes, such as tuition, fees, and room and board.

WHO KNEW?

About two-thirds of all full-time undergraduates receive financial aid in the form of grants.

STRATEGY TIP: BE THE LANDLORD OF ANIMAL HOUSE!

If you have college-age children and an appetite to own investment real estate, here's a strategy that can work on a number of levels. Buy a house, condo, or apartment building near your child's college campus, and have your child (and hopefully a roommate) pay you rent. Hire your child to maintain and manage the property. The salary you pay your child will be a tax deductible rental expense, just like property taxes, mortgage interest, repairs, depreciation, and other operating deductions that landlords are entitled to. Meanwhile, your child will pay income tax on the salary at their lower tax rates. Look at the benefits—your child has housing and a job, you shifted income to your child at a lower tax rate, and you have a tax-advantaged investment that is being watched over by somebody you can (hopefully) trust.

LIFETIME LEARNING CREDIT

The lifetime learning credit is a tax credit for any person who takes college classes. It provides a tax credit of up to $2,000 on the first $10,000 of college tuition and fees. You can claim the lifetime learning credit on your tax return if you, your spouse, or your dependents are enrolled at an eligible educational institution and you were responsible for paying college expenses. Unlike the American opportunity credit, you need not be enrolled at least half-time. Even if you took only one class, you may take advantage of the lifetime learning credit.

NOTES

YOUR JOB ^{chapter} 5

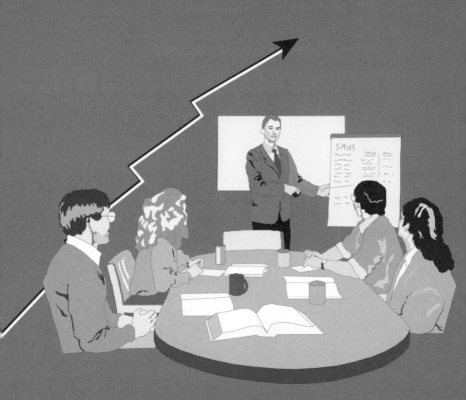

SEE YOU IN THE COMPANY CAFETERIA

A Cafeteria plan is an account you set up that takes money out of each paycheck before taxes are taken. The money can be used for approved medical and daycare costs. The significance of this plan is that the money is available to you during the year untaxed, and by removing it from your paycheck before taxes are figured, you end up paying less taxes than you would otherwise. For some people, a Cafeteria plan will increase the amount of cash available to them without decreasing their net paycheck at all.

ON THE FRINGE

How'd you like to avoid paying taxes on part of your pay? Certain fringe benefits provided by your employer and taken out of your paycheck are exempt from federal and state income tax. You don't even pay Social Security or Medicare tax on them. Some of the most common are:

• Health benefits, including health, dental, and vision insurance (most companies provide at least some of these!)
• Long-term care insurance
• Group term life insurance
• Disability insurance
• Tuition fees
• Daycare and other dependent care assistance
• Parking and mass transit costs

These pre-tax benefits can save you big. For example, employers can pay up to $230 per month for employee parking. If you were paying this amount out of your after-tax pay and are in the 33 percent tax bracket, you'd have to earn more than $400 in salary to bring home that $230 after federal taxes, Social Security, and FICA. If your company pays the $230 for parking and reduces your pre-tax salary by the same amount, you'll wind up with more money in your pocket at the end of the month.

If you are paying for any of the above fringe benefits on your own, out of your take-home pay, it's worth it to try negotiating with the boss to increase your benefits, even if it means reducing your salary. Not only will you save, but so will your company—they also don't have to pay their portion of Social Security and Medicare taxes on the part of your salary used for the benefits.

A BREAK FOR JOB HUNTERS

When you're job searching, it's important to keep track of your job search expenses, because these costs may be a tax deduction when you file your income taxes. You don't have to be out of work to have some of your costs qualify as a deductible expense, but only expenses that exceed 2 percent of your income count. If you've been looking for a job in the same line of work you're currently in, many of your expenses—like phone calls, the costs of preparing and copying your resume, and career counseling—are deductible, even if you do not get a new job. You cannot deduct these expenses if:

• You are looking for a job in a new occupation
• There was a long period of unemployment between the ending of your last job and your looking for a new one
• You are looking for a job for the first time

DEDUCTIBLE JOB-SEARCH EXPENSES

Make sure you're deducting all of your job-hunting expenses! The following are costs you can deduct if you meet all the criteria listed above:

• Employment and outplacement agency fees. If you are paying these expenses (rather than your previous employer), you can deduct any costs you incur.

• Résumés, cover letters, and other correspondence. You can deduct amounts you spend for typing, printing, and mailing copies of a résumés to prospective employers if you are looking for a new job in your present occupation.

• Travel and transportation expenses. If you go on a trip and look for a new job while you're there, you may be able to deduct travel expenses

to and from the area—as long as the purpose of the trip is primarily to look for a new job.
• Phone calls. Local and long distance phone calls to prospective employers are also deductible!

NEW TAX BREAK FOR THE UNEMPLOYED

If you're unemployed, here's a bit of good news: All or part of your unemployment benefits received in 2009 will be tax free, based on a new rule provided by the IRS. The American Recovery and Reinvestment Act states that the first $2,400 of unemployment insurance is exempt from tax for everyone. Therefore, if you're a married couple and you both are unemployed, you both get to take the exemption. After this amount, however, you owe taxes. If you are unemployed, you have the ability to withhold taxes from your unemployment so there will be no surprises at tax time. Many choose not to, keeping as much cash on-hand as possible, but make your decision carefully— you don't want to end up owing lots of taxes to the IRS at the end of the year.

WORKING FROM HOME?

With technology making it easier than ever for people to operate a business without going into an office, many taxpayers may be able to take a home office deduction. Below are important things you should know about claiming the home office deduction. For more information, see IRS Publication 587: Business Use of Your Home.
• Generally, in order to claim a business deduction for your home, you must use part of your home exclusively and regularly as a principal place of business, or as a place to meet or deal with patients, clients, or customers in the normal course of your business.
• The amount you can deduct depends on the percentage of your home that you used for business. For example, if you are self-employed and use 10 percent of the square footage of your house as your office, then you can only deduct 10 percent of your rent or mortgage.
• Your deduction for certain expenses will be limited if your gross income from your business is less than your total business expenses (i.e., if you are showing a loss).
• Different rules apply for claiming the home office deduction if you are not self-employed. For example, your working from home must be for the convenience of your employer. There are also special rules for qualified daycare providers and for persons storing business inventory or product samples.

DEDUCT EVEN MORE JOB EXPENSES

As an employee, there may be times when you end up paying for some work-related expenses out of your own pocket. If your employer does NOT reimburse you for the expenditures listed below, you can deduct them if you're itemizing your deductions, as long as they are "ordinary, necessary, and reasonable in amount." However, you can only deduct up to 2 percent of your adjusted gross income. Some allowable expenditures for deduction are:

• Dues to professional societies
• Union dues and expenses
• Tools and supplies used in your work
• Work clothes and uniforms (only if required and not suitable for everyday use)
• Work-related travel, transportation, meal, and entertainment expenses
• Education costs and relate directly to your work

WHO KNEW?

In the month of March 2009, more than 5.5 million people received unemployment benefits.

NOTES

RETIREMENT chapter 6

FROM THE IRS

TIPS FOR TAXPAYERS WHO OWE MONEY TO THE IRS

The vast majority of Americans get a tax refund from the IRS each spring, but what do you do if you are one of those who received a tax bill? Here are eight tips for taxpayers who owe money to the IRS.

1. If you get a bill for late taxes, you are expected to promptly pay the tax owed including any additional penalties and interest. If you are unable to pay the amount due, it is often in your best interest to get a loan to pay the bill in full rather than to make installment payments to the IRS. The interest rate on a credit card or bank loan may be lower than the combination of interest and penalties imposed by the Internal Revenue Code.

2. You can pay the balance owed by electronic funds transfer, check, money order, cashier's check or cash. To pay using electronic funds transfer you can take advantage of the Electronic Federal Tax Payment System by calling 800-555-4477 or 800-945-8400 or online at www.eftps.gov.

3. You can also pay the bill with your credit card. To pay by credit card contact either Official Payments Corporation at 800-2PAYTAX (also www.officialpayments.com) or Link2Gov at 888-PAY-1040 (also www.pay1040.com).

4. An installment agreement may be requested if you cannot pay the liability in full. This is an agreement between you and the IRS for the collection of the amount due in monthly installment payments. To be eligible for an installment agreement, you must first file all returns that are required and be current with estimated tax payments.

DON'T CASH OUT

The consequences of prematurely dipping into your retirement fund are steep. Do the math: A person in the 25 percent federal tax bracket who makes a $50,000 withdrawal before age 59½ will pay federal taxes of $12,500 on that money. Assuming a hypothetical 7 percent state tax, that's an additional $3,500 more than it would have been if the person was over 59½. Then, there's a 10 percent early withdrawal penalty ($5,000 in this case). So, after taxes and penalties, that $50,000 in retirement savings becomes $29,000 in your pocket. Ouch.

5. If you owe $25,000 or less in combined tax, penalties and interest, you can request an installment agreement using the web-based application called Online Payment Agreement found at IRS.gov.

6. You can also complete and mail an IRS Form 9465, Installment Agreement Request, along with your bill in the envelope that you have received from the IRS. The IRS will inform you usually within 30 days whether your request is approved, denied, or if additional information is needed. If the amount you owe is $25,000 or less, provide the monthly amount you wish to pay with your request. At a minimum, the monthly amount you will be allowed to pay without completing a Collection Information Statement (Form 433) is an amount that will full pay the total balance owed within sixty months.

7. You may still qualify for an installment agreement if you owe more than $25,000, but Form 433F (Collection Information Statement) is required to be completed before an installment agreement can be considered. If your balance is over $25,000, consider your financial situation and propose the highest amount possible, as that is how the IRS will arrive at your payment amount based upon your financial information.

8. If an agreement is approved, a one-time user fee will be charged. The user fee for a new agreement is $105 or $52 for agreements where payments are deducted directly from your bank account. For eligible individuals with incomes at or below certain levels, a reduced fee of $43 will be charged, and is automatically figured based on your income.

9. For more information about installment agreements and other payment options, see Publication 594: The IRS Collection Process and Publication 966: Electronic Choices to Pay All Your Federal Taxes.

WHO KNEW?

Less than 10 percent of Americans contribute enough to their 401(k)s to get the maximum company match. Don't follow the crowd in letting this free money fly out the window. For a worker making $50,000 and eligible for a full employer match of 50 cents to the dollar on 6 percent of his or her pay, that is $1,500 a year in free money available!

WHO KNEW?

According to Hewitt research, 45 percent of employees cash out their 401(k) plans when they leave a job. By not rolling it over to an IRA, they likely lose over 40 percent of the money to the tax man in the process. Don't make that mistake.

INVEST IN YOUR FUTURE

By now you know that your Social Security benefits, even with some retirement benefits from an employer (if you're lucky enough to have them), probably won't provide you with the financial security you'll want for your golden years. You know you need to save up so that you'll have assets to generate income for you. So the most valuable tax tip you'll ever get is this: put as much money as you can into tax advantaged retirement accounts, like 401(k)s or IRAs.

MAKE THE BOSS INVEST WITH YOU

Max out your employer plan! If your employer offers a 401(k) or 403(b), maximize your contributions as soon as you can. If you're lucky enough to have an employer that matches some or all of your contribution, be sure to put in at least enough to get all of the matching dollars. If you don't, you're throwing away free money! As if you needed an added bonus, the matching funds that are contributed by your employer are not taxable—they are considered a tax-free fringe benefit.

TAX FREE? THAT'S FOR ME!

A Roth IRA is one of the most exciting retirement opportunities available, particularly for younger investors. Unlike with a plain-vanilla IRA, you contribute to a Roth IRA after you pay taxes on it. Then, once you reach retirement, you won't owe any taxes on withdrawals. Strange as it may sound, one of our advisors suggested thinking of yourself as a farmer: "It's like paying tax on a seed and getting the harvest for free." Before you decide to open a Roth IRA, weigh your current tax rate against what you think your tax rate will be in the future. If you expect that you'll be in a higher tax bracket when you reach retirement, Roth is a good bet. But if you are making a ton of money now—and think your salary will likely be lower when you're close to retirement—you might want to delay taxes and stick with a traditional 401(k) or IRA. It's not an either-or decision, though. Consider hedging your bets by contributing to both. For example, if you're putting $5,000 a year into a 401(k), then it might be prudent to put another $5,000 into a Roth IRA. This way, half of your money tax-free now, and the other half is tax-free later. You never pay any taxes on the earnings in the account. In fact, you do not even report the income to the IRS. Even in retirement, when you ideally first access your Roth IRA money, you do not owe taxes on the distribution.

A CHOICE FOR RETIREES

Eventually the time comes when you say goodbye to the workplace and start taking money out of those retirement accounts you've been funding for so long. In exchange for the tax deferral benefits that Uncle Sam gives you on these accounts, there are some rules regarding withdrawals that must be followed. The big rules are about timing—you can't start too soon or too late.

• Too soon: You're not supposed to make any withdrawals from retirement accounts until you're 59½. Otherwise, not only will you have to pay the regular income tax on the withdrawal, you'll have a 10 percent federal penalty (unless an exception applies).

THANKS, MR. ROTH!

Unlike 401(k) plans and traditional IRAs, there is no age at which you must begin to distribute money from your Roth IRA. As a result, Roth IRAs are an excellent tool to pass along wealth to your children or grandchildren.

• Too late: Starting at age 70½, you are required to take a certain amount out each year and pay tax on it (except for Roth accounts). Required minimum distributions (RMDs) are the minimum amounts that the IRS says a person over the age of 70½ must withdraw annually. Because the value of many retirement accounts fell drastically in the stock market meltdown at the end of 2008, Congress has temporarily suspended these rules for 2009. This means that although you're allowed to take as much out of your IRA as you want, you are not required to withdraw any amount. RMDs will come back in 2010 and will be based on account values as of December 31, 2009.

SELF-EMPLOYED? OPEN A SEP-IRA

If you're a small business owner, a SEP-IRA (Simplified Employee Pension-Individual Retirement Account) is an easy-to-administer retirement plan that allows you to put aside money in a tax-deferred account for retirement. As a sole proprietor or LLC member, you can contribute 20 percent of your profits from self-employment (net profit minus one half of your self-employment tax), up to a limit of $49,000 for 2009. This is a great way to really build up some retirement funds in a short period of time.

INVESTMENTS chapter 7

WHO KNEW?

Under federal law, you generally pay tax at a lower rate on your first dollar of income than you do on your last dollar. The highest rate at which your income is taxed—called your "marginal rate"—is used to calculate taxes on your investment income.

GO LONG

To encourage people to make long-term investments, long-term capital gains receive the most favorable treatment and are taxed at the lowest rates. Through the end of 2010, if your taxable income is under $32,550 (or $65,100 if filing jointly), your long-term capital gains tax is zero! If your income is above those thresholds, your rate is only 15 percent. The best way to take advantage of these historically low rates is to manage both your losses and your gains.

AN OLDIE BUT GOODIE

A simple way to defer income is to purchase US savings bonds. You don't have to pay any federal income taxes on the interest earned on I bonds or series EE savings bonds until you cash them in or it stops earning interest 30 years from the issue date. This tax deferral feature is automatic, so you don't have to do anything to get it, and this interest is not subject to state or local tax. An added bonus is that you may not have to pay any federal tax on the interest if you use the money from these bonds to pay for higher education expenses for yourself or someone else.

AVOID THE EARLY WITHDRAWAL PAIN

If you cash in a CD or savings account before its fixed maturity date, you may have to pay a penalty. This penalty is subtracted from the funds you receive. You can deduct this penalty, even if you don't itemize deductions; however, better to avoid the penalty in the first place. When putting money into these time-savings vehicles, don't extend the maturity beyond the time you might need the funds. Consider splitting your savings into multiple certificates with different maturity dates so that you can readily have access to some funds free of penalty.

WHAT A CAPITAL IDEA

Anytime you sell something you own—a house, a share of stock, bonds, or your Babe Ruth baseball card—that is a capital sale. If you sell it at a profit, it is classified as a capital gain. Conversely, if you sell at a loss it is a capital loss. Tax rates on capital gains can be significantly lower than tax rates on ordinary income—in some cases as low as 5 or even 0 percent. The tax rate depends on how long you owned the asset (known as your holding period). If you own an asset for at least one year before you sell it, any profit or loss you receive from the sale is considered a long-term capital gain or loss. If you hold it for less than a year, any gain or loss is a short-term capital gain or loss.

HAVE THE COMBO PLATTER! A INSURANCE/INVESTMENT/TAX SHELTER

Life insurance policies that combine investments with insurance (like whole life or universal life) enjoy substantial tax-favored status. Part of your premium is invested. Earnings on the cash value are not taxed until you cash in the policy. If the policy is in force when you die, the proceeds go to your beneficiary completely free of any federal income tax. These factors combine to produce a powerful tax and estate planning tool with the following benefits:

• Tax-free death benefit. The death benefits of life insurance policies are free from all federal income taxes. The enormous value of this benefit must not be underestimated, especially in light of constantly growing government expenditures and taxes.

• Tax-deferred growth. The growth of cash value inside of the life insurance policy is deferred from taxes while the funds remain in the policy. This is yet another wealth-protecting benefit for families and businesses provided by whole life Insurance.

• Tax-favorable access to the policy's cash value by withdrawing dividends. During the insured's life, cash values can be accessed under favorable FIFO (First-In-First-Out) tax rules. The IRS assumes that the first money pulled out is a return of your premiums rather than the earnings, however, additional withdrawals are considered taxable income. This means that dividend withdrawals are tax-free up to the amount of premium paid cumulatively.

TURNAROUND TACTIC

Believe your stocks will turn around? One option is to sell shares for a tax loss and then, after a mandatory waiting period of more than thirty days, buy the same ones again. To avoid the month-long wait, you can look for shares to immediately buy in a different but comparable firm; mutual fund investors often can switch among similar funds within the same fund group.

• Tax-favorable access to policy cash value through policy loans. During the insured's life, loans taken against a life insurance policy will not trigger a taxable event, even though the policy may have a large gain in excess of the premiums paid.

BE A GRACIOUS WINNER
Assuming you're fortunate enough to have gains you want to cash in on, the good news for sales before year-end is that you typically pay a top rate of either 0 or 15 percent on gains from stock held longer than a year. That long-term capital-gains rate may be worth grabbing now; some investors fear it will go up when Congress starts to look at the costs of the many recent stimulus programs. You could even buy back the same stock; because you sold at a gain, no 30-day waiting period is required.

MAKE MINE A DOUBLE
Instead of making charitable contributions in cash, you should consider donating securities (that is, shares of stocks, mutual funds, or bonds) that have appreciated in value and that you've owned for longer than one year. This can give you a rare "double dip" bonus in tax savings: 1. You can generally take a tax deduction for the full market value of the securities (rather than the amount you paid), and 2. You avoid paying capital gains tax on the amount the securities have appreciated since you bought them—a tax you would've had to pay if you sold the securities first and then donated the cash proceeds. For example, instead of writing a check for $1,000 to your favorite charity, you tell your broker to give them $1,000 worth of your Apple stock. Even though you may have only paid $200 for it, you still get a tax deduction for $1,000 and you never have to pay tax on the $800 gain. That's the double dip.

BE A GOOD LOSER
It's easy to find losses in most stock portfolios these days, so why not make those lemons into lemonade? Losses you take on sales before the end of the year can offset any taxable gains you rang up earlier—and also offset up to $3,000 a year of wages and other taxable income. Leftover losses can be carried over to offset taxable income in future years.

DEDUCTING FOR TRAVEL

chapter 8

BUSINESS TRAVEL

Any form of travel or lodging for business that is ordinary and necessary can be claimed as a business deduction. For example, if you are on an overnight business trip and your client has a last-minute, urgent meeting and must push yours back to the following day, it is a necessary reason to stay another night. The cost of the room, taxi or airport shuttle, plane fare, and associated costs are all deductible business expenses. Also, the travel doesn't have to be yours to qualify. Flying a potential employee to see your company or a client to your offices are examples of valid travel deductions. All expenses in relation to these visits are deductible!

FROM THE IRS

THE LUCKY SEVEN: TAX TIPS FOR GAMBLING WINNINGS AND LOSSES

You may know when to hold 'em and when to fold 'em, but do you know how and when to report 'em? Whether you are playing cards or the slots, it is important to know the rules about reporting gambling winnings and losses. Here are seven things the IRS wants you to know about reporting what Lady Luck has sent your way.

1. All gambling winnings are fully taxable.

2. Gambling income includes, but is not limited to, winnings from lotteries, raffles, horse races, poker tournaments, and casinos. It includes cash winnings and also the fair market value of prizes such as cars and trips.

3. A payer is required to issue you a Form W-2G if you receive certain gambling winnings or if you have any gambling winnings subject to federal income tax withholding.

4. Even if a W-2G is not issued, all gambling winnings must be reported as taxable income. Therefore, you may be required to pay an estimated tax on the gambling winnings. For more information on paying estimated taxes, refer to Publication 505: Tax Withholding and Estimated Tax.

5. You must report your gambling winnings on Form 1040, line 21.

6. If you itemize your deductions on Form 1040, Schedule A, you can deduct gambling losses you had during the year, but only up to the amount of your winnings. Your losses are not subject to the 2 percent of AGI limitation.

7. It is important to keep an accurate diary or similar record of your gambling winnings and losses. To deduct your losses, you must be able to provide receipts, tickets, statements, or other records that show the amount of both your winnings and losses.

DON'T RAISE THE FLAG

When it comes to traveling and entertaining for business, expenses must be well-documented so that no red flags get raised on your tax return. It would be great to take a trip to Paris and write it all off on our taxes, but that's only possible if the trip complies with IRS laws. Basically, for travel and entertainment expenses to be considered as deductions, they must be ordinary and necessary for your business. "Ordinary" means that they are part of what is considered normal for your type of business. If you're a doctor, talking business with a client in a nightclub may be a bit of a stretch. Deducting the cost of a meal in a fancy restaurant, however, may not. Business can ordinarily be discussed in that setting and, of course, both of you have to eat.

"Necessary" means that it is something that is helpful for your business. Traveling to California to meet with a client who lives out there is necessary. Taking your family with you (and then trying to deduct the expense) is not. Any travel or entertainment expense that's used for business and personal reasons must be divided proportionately and accurately for the purpose of business deductions.

ENTERTAINING

When looking to deduct entertainment expenses, make sure they are necessary and ordinary. Showing a client a night on the town while he is in your city may qualify as an entertainment expense that can be deducted on your taxes. Meals with a client during which business is discussed can also be deducted as a travel expense when visiting the client. However, a trip to Disneyland with your client is probably not. Furthermore, when tax time rolls around it's important to remember to deduct each event only once. For example, if you deduct your meals on an overnight trip as travel expenses, don't try to use the same meals to claim a deduction for entertainment expenses.

DEDUCTIBLE VACATION

While not everyone will be able to justify that weekend in Rome, a professional translator would certainly be able to justify the trip as a business related expense for maintaining language skills. Many trips can be tax deductible. Meet with potential clients, hold a couple of conferences, have lunch with a client while you're there, and you can write off a portion of your travel expenses to reduce your tax burden.

ROLL THE DICE ON A VACATION

If you happen to find yourself in the lucky position of having net gambling winnings near the end of the year, maybe it's a good time to treat yourself to a gambling vacation. Net winnings are taxable (and can only be offset by gambling losses), but net loses are deductible. So if you lose on your trip, you'll be able to write it off. And if you happen to win on vacation, well just consider it your lucky year.

GOOD RECORDS CAN SAVE THE DAY

There's a wide degree of latitude for travel and business expenses, but the rule of thumb is to document *everything*. Keep an organizer that lists the dates of your trip along with an envelope for all receipts; this will ensure that no deductible expenses are missed. Consult a tax professional if you have any questions regarding the validity of an expense. If you can prove that business was conducted, the expense should stand.

GET ME TO A DOCTOR

The law lets you treat travel costs for medical purposes as a deductible medical expense. Sorry, but this doesn't cover going to Florida for the winter to escape the cold of New Jersey, even if the warm weather is better for you! Some examples of acceptable medical travel costs are:

- The expense of an ambulance
- Bus, cab, or train fare (or automobile use at 24¢ per mile) to a doctor's office, pharmacy, treatment center, and even programs like AA meetings
- Costs to get to and attend a medical conference on an illness or condition suffered by you, your spouse, or a dependent
- Lodging to receive outpatient care at a hospital or clinic for up to $50 per night, or $100 per night if you accompany a sick child.

HELLO, MY NAME IS_____

Conventions and trade shows are an important way for businesses to show off their products, make new connections, and learn about developments in their industry. Whether you're a visitor or an exhibitor, your attendance costs may be deductible if they are not reimbursed by your employer, or if you are self-employed. Be aware that there are limitations if you attend a convention held outside of North America or on a cruise ship.

BORROWING & INTEREST

chapter 9

WHO KNEW?

The sixteenth amendment to the Constitution, ratified in 1913, established the first permanent income tax in the US. Four states—Florida, Utah, Connecticut, and Rhode Island—rejected the amendment.

DEDUCTION, SWEET DEDUCTION

As we discussed in Chapter 3, Your Home, mortgage interest on a loan secured by your home (either a primary residence or a second home) is deductible. Whether the loan is a mortgage, investment loan, or home equity loan, if you use the funds to buy, build, or improve upon your main or second home, it's called a home acquisition loan. You can deduct the annual interest you pay on acquisition loans of up to $1 million. If you use the loan secured by your home for other purposes, it's a home equity loan, and you can deduct the annual interest you pay on loans of up to $100,000.

If you paid points on your loan, figuring your deduction is a little trickier. Generally, if you took out a mortgage to buy, build, or improve upon your main home, you can deduct the points in the year you paid them. If you refinance, however, you can only deduct them a little at a time, over the life of the new loan.

CONSOLIDATE IS GREAT (BUT ONLY IF YOU GET STRAIGHT)

If you are a homeowner with a significant balance of high-interest credit card debt, and substantial equity in your home, you can save big on interest expense by consolidating your credit cards with a home equity loan, while also making the interest expense deductible. CAUTION: Only do this if you are willing to cut up the credit cards at the same time! Assuming it wasn't a medical or severe emergency that brought about the high balances, your inability to manage them is what got you in trouble. If you consolidate and go back to you old ways, then all you've done is turn unsecured credit card debt into secured debt (i.e., now the bank can take your house!) If you've learned your lesson about credit card spending and what to pay less in interest, consider taking out a home equity loan to pay off the cards, then cancel the accounts.

The after-tax interest cost savings can be dramatic. For example, if you have a total balance of $40,000 on credit cards averaging 18 percent interest, you pay $7,200 per year in non-deductible interest on that debt. If you pay them off with a home equity loan of the same amount at 6 percent interest, your interest expense drops to $2,400. Better yet, it becomes deductible, so that if you're in the 30 percent tax bracket, your effective after-tax interest expense is $1,680— a savings of $5,520 per year!

VISA MAY FORGIVE YOU, BUT THE IRS WON'T

This economy has been a nightmare. No one's job is safe, people are losing their homes, and others are relying on their credit cards to make ends meet. Credit card companies are also feeling the pain of rising delinquencies and are responding by settling delinquent accounts for a fraction of what is owed. Why do they do this? That's easy—collection activities cost credit card companies money. They have to pay for all the letters and notices, and the person calling you to nag about payments, and even then they probably won't recover all the money you owe. So, when a customer offers a lump sum payment to settle the entire debt, many companies are jumping at the chance. Whatever balance is not covered by the lump sum, the credit card company just forgives. While this is great for consumers in the short-term, it will cost you some money down the road.

Aside from the damage done to your credit score, there is a potentially bigger problem laying in wait for you next tax season. If your credit card

INTERESTED?
To get your home mortgage loan, you may have paid all sorts of charges not labeled as interest, like origination fees, maximum loan charges, and premium charges. If any of these charges were solely for the use of the money and not for a specific service (like an appraisal), then good news—they're considered prepaid interest and can be deducted. Check your closing statement.

CONGRESS LEFT THE DOOR OPEN FOR YOU

Most home buyers who can't afford a 20 percent down payment must pay private mortgage insurance (PMI) to protect lenders against default. If you've paid PMI, a 2006 tax law gives you a deduction that will take some of the pain out of your monthly payments. (This deduction was scheduled to expire at the end of 2007, but Congress voted to extend it through 2010.) To qualify for the deduction you must have bought or refinanced your home after January 1, 2007. Families with adjusted gross incomes of up to $100,000 can deduct 100 percent of their insurance premiums, much the same as they deduct property taxes. The annual premiums run about 0.5 to 0.75 percent of the outstanding balance, $500 to $750 a year for every $100,000 you owe.

company didn't make you pay part of what you owe them, the IRS calls that "Forgiven Debt," and it may be reported to the IRS as taxable income. So if you settle your $25,000 Visa bill for only $5,000, the "forgiven" twenty grand is now considered income. If you're in the 15 percent tax bracket, that will mean your tax bill will increase by $3,000. The increased "income" can even bump you up into a higher tax bracket!

BUH-BYE, PMI

If you didn't have 20 percent equity in your home at the time of taking out your mortgage, you're probably paying PMI. But are you paying for PMI that you don't need? Once you cross that 20 percent threshold, you may be able to drop that insurance. For example, say you bought your house two years ago for $600,000, with $100,000 down payment and a thirty-year mortgage at 5 percent for the $500,000 balance. Meanwhile, you're paying PMI with an annual premium of $4,200 per year. In the two years since you bought the house, the mortgage has been paid down to a balance of about $485,000. If your home has appreciated just a little bit over the same period, to approxmiately $610,000, guess what? You now have over 20 percent equity in your home, and may be able to drop that PMI policy, **saving $4,200 per year!** Contact your loan servicer.

IS FORGIVEN DEBT ALWAYS TAXABLE?

Not always. There are some exceptions, especially if your debt is mortgage-backed. The most common situations when cancellation of debt income is not taxable involve:

• Qualified principal residence indebtedness. This is the exception created by the Mortgage Debt Relief Act of 2007 and applies to most homeowners.

• Bankruptcy: Debts discharged through bankruptcy are not considered taxable income.

• Insolvency: If you are insolvent when the debt is cancelled, some or all of the cancelled debt may not be taxable. (You are insolvent when your total debts are more than the fair market value of your total assets.)

• Certain farm debts: If you incurred the debt directly because of the operation of a farm, more than half your income from the prior three years was from farming, and the loan was owed to a person or agency regularly engaged in lending, your cancelled debt is not considered taxable income.

• Non-recourse loans: A non-recourse loan is a loan for which the lender's only remedy in case of default is to repossess the property being financed or used as collateral. That is, the lender cannot pursue you personally in case of default. Forgiveness of a non-recourse loan resulting from a foreclosure does not result in cancellation of debt income. However, it may result in other tax consequences.

NOTES

OTHER TIPS, TRICKS, & TRAPS

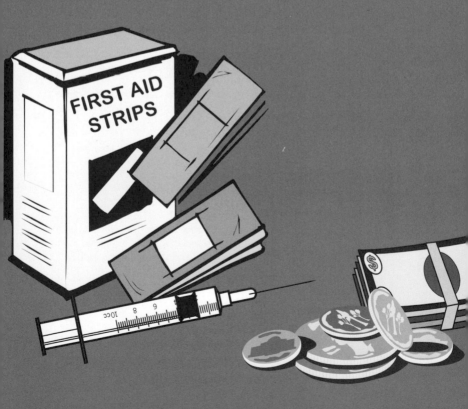

FROM THE IRS

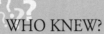

WHO KNEW?

It could be worse. Peter the Great of Russia taxed beards. There was also a tax on souls, hats, basements, and beehives.

TEN THINGS YOU MAY NOT KNOW ABOUT THE EARNED INCOME TAX CREDIT

The earned income tax credit (EITC) is for people who work, but have lower incomes. Here are some things you may not know about the EITC.

1.   A quarter of all taxpayers that qualify don't claim the credit. The EITC is money you can use to make a difference in your life. Just because you didn't qualify last year, doesn't mean you won't this year. As your financial situation changes from year to year, you should review the EITC eligibility rules to determine if you qualify.

2.   If you qualify, it could be worth up to $4,800 in 2009. If you qualify, you could pay less federal tax or even get a refund. The EITC is based on the amount of your earned income and whether or not there are qualifying children in your household.

3.   Your filing status cannot be married filing separately. Your filing status must be married filing jointly, head of household, qualifying widow, or single.

4.   You must have a valid Social Security Number. You, your spouse (if filing a joint return), and any qualifying child listed on Schedule EIC must have a valid SSN issued by the Social Security Administration.

5.   You must have earned income. This credit is called the "earned income" tax credit because you must work and have earned income to qualify. You have earned income if you work for someone who pays you wages or you are self-employed.

6. Married couples and single people without kids may qualify. If you do not have qualifying children, you must also meet the age and residency requirements as well as dependency rules.

7. Special rules apply to members of the US Armed Forces in combat zones. Members of the military can elect to include their nontaxable combat pay in earned income for the EITC. If you make the election, the combat pay remains nontaxable, but you must include in earned income all nontaxable combat pay you received.

8. You can visit the IRS Web site to estimate your credit online. It's easy to determine whether you qualify for the EITC. The EITC Assistant, an interactive tool available on IRS.gov, removes the guesswork from eligibility rules. Just answer a few simple questions to find out if you qualify and to estimate the amount of your EITC. You will see the results of your responses right away.

9. E-file programs will figure the credit for you. If you are preparing your taxes electronically, the software program you use will figure the credit for you.

10. You don't have to wait until you file your tax return to receive your EITC. Advance EITC is a portion of the EITC that qualified workers may be able to receive in advance payments, added to their wages throughout the year. For more information, see Form W-5: Earned Income Credit Advance Payment Certificate.

11. For more information about the EITC and Advance EITC see IRS Publication 596: Earned Income Credit.

WHEN IN DOUBT, CHECK 'EM OUT

You can ask any organization you're donating to whether it's a qualified organization for deducting your donation. They should be able to give you a copy of a letter from the IRS saying so. You can also check the website Guidestar. org. They list over a million qualified charities and contain in-depth financial information about them.

WHEN IT'S SMART TO PAY EARLY

It may seem crazy to pay your taxes before they're due, but it may be worth it. State income taxes paid are an itemized tax deduction on your federal return. Many people can benefit by paying their state income taxes before year end in order to maximize their deductions for federal taxes. Be careful, though, as this strategy can possibly throw you into AMT (alternative minimum tax). If you plan on prepaying a substantial amount of state tax, consult with a tax advisor to make sure this strategy will work for you.

IT ADDS UP!

Keep in mind, there are a lot of things you may not think of as medical expenses, but are deductible. If an elderly parent qualifies as your dependent, you can deduct your out-of-pocket expenses for their medical care, which can really add up. In addition, the broad IRS definition of medical expenses includes any payment for "the diagnosis, cure, mitigation, treatment, or prevention of disease, or treatment affecting any structure or function of the body." That's a pretty wide net. Aside from money spent on doctors, dentists, nursing care, lab fees, hospitals, and long term care, that definition includes much more. For example, IRS-recognized medical expenses include fees paid to psychiatrists, chiropractors, optometrists, acupuncturists, and much more. You can also deduct transportation costs for treatment, or the cost of renovating your home to accommodate a handicap (like a wheelchair ramp). To learn more about deducting your medical and dental expenses, see IRS Publication 502: Medical and Dental Expenses.

WHAT IS THIS AMT? WHY DO I CARE?

The AMT, or Alternative Minimum Tax, is designed to force taxpayers to pay a minimum amount of tax, even if they would pay less tax under the regular tax rules. The AMT was originally created to prevent people with high incomes from paying very little taxes by using shelters, but it now affects more low-income people than it does people in the highest tax brackets. More and more people are getting caught in the AMT trap, and many tax preparers are not aware of the strategies that can be used to legally avoid AMT. Some of these strategies can be done when the tax return is prepared, but others need to be done before the end of the year. Visit IRS.gov and type "AMT" into the search box for an "assistant" that will help you figure it you qualify for the AMT. If so, ask your tax professional if he or she has experience with alternative minimum tax.

BUNDLE UP

"Bundling" medical expenses can maximize your deduction. This idea behind this strategy is to pile on your expenses every other year, thereby giving yourself the maximum deduction for that year. To do this just requires a bit of simple planning. Each year calculate an estimate of what 7.5 percent of your adjusted gross income will be. Then keep a running total of your out-of-pocket medical expenses as they accumulate. If you start to near your threshold, determine if there are expenses planned for next year that you can accelerate to bundle into the current calendar year. Think of elective surgery or expensive dental

WHO KNEW IT'S SHOPPING SEASON?

Many states temporarily waive sales tax on clothing or other items for a week or two at different times during the year, especially during the summer or right before school starts. For more information on states and dates, go to Taxadmin.org/fta/rate/sales_holiday.html.

procedures like orthodontia. Maybe you could stock up on prescription medicines, or get new eyeglasses. On the other hand, if you are not close to your threshold, then hold off on any elective expenses until the next year. This way you can effectively bunch expenses into one year to exceed the 7.5 percent floor.

DON'T BE LAZY—IT COULD COST YOU!

Because of the 7.5% limitation on deducting medical expenses, many people assume they'll never be able to deduct them, so they don't bother going through the trouble of keeping track. This is a bad idea for several reasons! First, you could end up being wrong, perhaps because of a medical emergency late in the year. Secondly, even if you don't exceed the federal threshold of 7.5 percent, your state may have a lower threshold, or even no threshold at all. And finally, not knowing what your expenses are late in the year deprives you of the ability to utilize the planning strategy of bundling expenses in one taxable year. You could wind up giving up a valuable deduction without even knowing it, or without having the proper records to support it.

VOLUNTEERS OF AMERICA

Almost one quarter of Americans do some kind of volunteer work each year. While the individuals bear the burden of their time and efforts, the IRS is willing to help defray any out-of-pocket costs through a deduction. This is one of the most overlooked deductions! Examples include materials and supplies you provide, invitations, food, beverages, telephone costs, and travel expenses. If you use your vehicle for charitable purposes you can deduct 14¢ per mile.

FROM THE IRS

I THINK I CAN, I THINK I CAN: LAST MINUTE FILING TIPS

If the tax filing deadline is close at hand, the IRS offers these ten tips for those still working on their tax returns.

1. File electronically. Consider filing electronically instead of using paper tax forms. If you file electronically and choose direct deposit, you can receive your refund in as few as ten days.

2. Check the identification numbers. When filing a paper return carefully check the identification numbers—usually Social Security Numbers—for each person listed. This includes you, your spouse, dependents, and persons listed in relation to claims for the child and dependent care. Missing, incorrect, or illegible Social Security Numbers can delay or reduce a tax refund.

3. Double-check your figures. If you are filing a paper return, you should double-check that you have correctly figured the refund or balance due.

4. Check the tax tables. Make sure that you have used the right figure from the tax table that relates to your gross adjusted income.

5. Sign your form. Taxpayers must sign and date their returns. Both spouses must sign a joint return, even if only one had income. Anyone paid to prepare a return must also sign it.

6. Mailing your return. Use the coded envelope included with your tax package to mail your return. If you did not receive an envelope, check the section called "Where Do You File?" in the tax instruction booklet.

7. Mailing a payment. People sending a payment should make the check out to "United States Treasury" and should enclose it with, but not attach it to, the tax return or the Form 1040-V: Payment Voucher. The check should include the taxpayer's Social Security Number,

daytime phone number, the tax year, and the type of form filed.

8. Electronic payments: Electronic payment options are convenient, safe, and secure methods for paying taxes. You can authorize an electronic funds withdrawal, or use a credit card or a debit card. For more information on electronic payment options, visit IRS.gov.

9. Extension to file. By the April due date, taxpayers should either file a return or request an extension of time to file. Remember, the extension of time to file is not an extension of time to pay.

10 IRS.gov. Forms and publications and helpful information on a variety of tax subjects are available around the clock on the IRS website at IRS.gov.

STILL WORKING AT 11:45 P.M. ON APRIL 15?

If you can't meet the April filing deadline to file your tax return, you can get an automatic six month extension of time to file from the IRS. Here is what you need to know about filing an extension:

• An extension will give you extra time to get your paperwork to the IRS, but it doesn't extend the time you have to pay any tax due. You'll also owe interest on any amount not paid by the April deadline, plus a late payment charge if it amount already withheld doesn't cover t least 90 percent of your total tax.

• If you finished filled out your return, but are unable to pay the full amount of tax due, don't request an extension. Instead, go ahead and file your return on time and pay as much as you can. The IRS will send you a bill for the balance due. To apply online for a payment agreement, go to IRS.gov and use the pull-down menu under "I need to…" to select "Set Up a Payment Plan." If you are unable to make payments, call the IRS at 800-829-1040 to discuss your payment options.

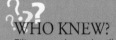

WHO KNEW?

Filing over the web will also help reduce mistakes. A reported 21 percent of paper returns have errors, whereas only 0.5 percent of e-file returns have errors.

MY MISTAKE—NOW WHAT?

So what *can* you do when your refund is sent to the wrong bank account? Verify the direct deposit information on your tax return versus the actual information from your bank. If the numbers you indicated on your tax return are correct, then call the IRS can ask them to initiate a refund trace to recover your refund. If the numbers you indicated on your tax return are incorrect, then you'll need to deal directly with the bank in which your refund was deposited. You'll know which bank and bank account it is, since you have the bank numbers listed on your tax return!

• Go to Routingnumbers.org and find the bank where the money was deposited by looking up which bank is associated with the routing number you entered on your tax return.

• Call the bank and ask to speak with the ACH manager.

• Next comes the tricky part. You have to persuade the bank to sent the refund back to the IRS. Explain the situation and hope for the best.

• Call the IRS (1-800-829-1040) and explain that the bank will be sending back the refund.

• Ask the IRS agent to fill out a Taxpayer Advocate Service Request (Form 911) to route your case to the taxpayer advocate.

• When the advocate contacts you, explain that you want this incident added to their annual report as a direct deposit error.

• In the future, always get a check, unless you are 100 percent sure that your bank info is correct!

• To request an extension, you'll still need to submit Form 4868 (Application for Automatic Extension of Time to File U.S. Individual Income Tax Return) by April 15. You can also e-file an extension request using tax preparation software such as TurboTax.

• If you ask for an extension via computer, you can also choose to pay any expected balance due by authorizing an direct debit from your checking or savings account. You'll need the appropriate bank routing and account numbers, and must also know the adjusted gross income from your previous year's federal income tax return to verify your identity.

I'M TAKING THE FREEWAY

Free File, a form of e-filing your taxes, is a free federal tax preparation and electronic filing program that you can access at IRS.gov. By visiting their site, you can fill out forms and electronically "sign" them, print them out for your records, and then submit your taxes through the computer. People who e-file normally receive tax refunds sooner, so this is a great system to check out.

WHAT I REALLY WANT TO DO IS DIRECT

Direct Deposit of your refund is a free service offered by the IRS and state tax agencies. Your tax preparer cannot charge you extra fees for using direct deposit. (This is forbidden by Treasury regulations governing tax professionals.) What do you need to know regarding direct deposit?

• Direct deposit is generally safer. Since there's no check to get lost in the mail or stolen by someone else, getting your refund by direct deposit is considered safer. However, you must make sure your bank information is 100 percent accurate.

• Direct deposits are send out earlier than paper checks. Direct deposit is faster because the IRS puts through direct deposits earlier than they mail out paper checks. Generally, the IRS transmits direct deposits a full seven days before they mail out a paper check.

• Double-check your direct deposit information. Make sure your bank routing number and account number you listed in the direct deposit section of your tax return are correct. These numbers are just as important as double-checking your name, address, and Social Security Number. If you aren't sure what your bank numbers are, call your bank and ask.

• What happens if you've accidentally put down the wrong bank information? You should verify your bank account information before sending in your tax return. However, if you discover a mistake in the direct deposit area you should call the IRS immediately at 1-800-829-1040 and ask that the IRS convert the refund to a paper check. Otherwise, the IRS will assume that the information you put in the direct deposit area is correct and will initiate the direct deposit in as little as eight days. If you don't catch them, there is probably no recourse through the government: the IRS has said that "the IRS assumes no responsibility for taxpayer error" as a result of inaccurate direct deposit information. Many taxpayers have reported losing their entire tax refunds simply by entering incorrect data.

GLOSSARY AND TAX CALCULATIONS

Throughout this book you'll find examples of savings based on amounts such as adjusted gross income, taxable income, deductions, and credits. Below is an illustration of how tax is calculated to give you a better idea of what these terms mean. In this example, Joe and Mary are a married couple with two young children, and they file a joint tax return. Joe earned $70,000 in salary from his job, while Mary earned $12,000 from a part-time home business, and they received $5,000 in interest income for their investments. Their total itemized deductions are $13,000, which exceeds their $10,900 standard deduction, making it worthwhile for them to itemize. Together they contributed $10,000 to their IRAs. They also received a tax credit of $2,000 for buying a hybrid car. Here's how they would compute their taxes:

$87,000	GROSS INCOME
– $10,000	Minus: Adjustments to income (IRA contributions)
$77,000	ADJUSTED GROSS INCOME (AGI)
– $13,000	Minus: Itemized deductions
– $14,000	Minus: Exemptions (4 people × $3,500)
$50,000	TAXABLE INCOME
– $ 6,710	Tax liability
– $ 2,000	Minus: Tax credits (hybrid vehicle)
$ 4,710	TAX DUE

Acquisition loan. Debt incurred to acquire, construct, or improve the taxpayer's principal or secondary residence.

After-tax amount. A figure that takes into account the tax cost or savings of an expense or benefit. Example: If a $1,000 expense is deductible, and the taxpayer is in the 30 percent tax bracket, the deduction of that expense will save him $300 in taxes. The after-tax cost of that expense is $700 ($1,000 expense minus $300).

Adjusted gross income (AGI). Gross income (the amount you made before taxes) minus any allowable adjustments, such as IRA, alimony, and certain other deductions. AGI determines whether various tax benefits are phased out, such as personal exemptions, itemized deductions, and the rental loss allowance.

Alternative minimum tax (AMT). A method of computing tax under which some of the income and deductions reported on the forms and schedules filed with your tax return are figured differently or disallowed. For example, certain itemized deductions are not allowed when figuring the alternative minimum tax, and the alternative minimum tax has its own exemption amount, not based on the number of exemptions claimed on your tax return. A taxpayer pays the larger of the "regular tax" or the alternative minimum tax.

Appreciation. Increase in value of an asset. When you sell appreciated property, you pay tax on the amount that its value has increased since the date of purchase. When you donate appreciated property held long term, you may generally deduct the appreciated value.

Asset. An item of useful or valuable property, like a share of stock, a bank account, a house, a car, or anything else you own that can be taxed.

Bundle. To group together the purchase of expenses into one calendar year. Example: If you're trying to increase your medical expense deduction for the year, you may want to buy three months of prescription medicines and a new pair of eyeglasses in December that you would have normally bought in January. You are "bundling" your medical expenses into the current year.

Cancellation of debt. Release of a debt without consideration by a creditor. Cancellations of debt are generally taxable.

Capital gain/loss. The difference between the sale price and the cost basis on the sale of capital assets. Long-term capital gains are taxed favorably. Capital losses are deducted first against capital gains, and then again up to $3,000 of other income.

Casualty. A casualty is the complete or partial destruction of property resulting from an identifiable event of a sudden, unexpected, or unusual nature. Examples are floods, storms, fires, earthquakes, and auto accidents.

Charitable deduction. Money or property donated to a qualified charitable organization. Such donations are deductible, subject to income limits, on Schedule A as itemized deductions.

Cost basis. The amount assigned to an asset from which gain or loss is determined for income tax purposes when the asset is sold. For assets acquired by purchase, basis is cost. Special rules govern the basis of property received by virtue of another's death or by gift. See also Stepped up basis.

Credit. See Tax credit

Custodian. See UGMA and UTMA

Debt consolidation. The strategy of paying off a group of debts (like credit cards) by taking out one new loan, presumably on better terms (like a home equity loan).

Deduction. Categories of expenses directly reducing income. Personal deductions such as for mortgage interest, state and local taxes, and charitable contributions are allowed only if deductions are itemized on Schedule A. Other types of expenses, such as alimony, capital losses, student loan interest, and IRA deductions are subtracted from gross income even if itemized deductions are not claimed. Any expense that is allowable as a deduction is said to be "deductible." Any expense that is NOT allowable as a deduction is said to be "non-deductible."

Deferral, tax. To defer taxes is to put off the payment of the taxes to a future year. Something that allows you to defer your tax bill is said to provide a "tax deferral." An example is contributing to a retirement account—the contribution is deductible, but when you take the money out in the future, you will pay taxes. You deferred some of your tax bill to your retirement.

Dependent. A child, relative, or household member for whom you support and an exemption may be claimed.

Depreciation. Depreciation is the deduction for the reasonable allowance for the wear and tear of assets with a life of more than one year, including real estate but not inventory, used in a trade or business or held for the production of income.

Earned income. Earned income is income for services rendered as distinguished from income generated by property or other sources. Earned income includes amounts received as wages, tips, bonuses, other employee compensation, and self-employment income.

Earned income tax credit (EITC). A refundable tax credit for qualified taxpayers based on earned income, adjusted gross income, and the number of qualifying children.

Estate. This term is most commonly used for a taxable entity that is established upon the death of a taxpayer. It consists of all the decedent's property and personal effects.

Exclusion. An amount of income that is not included in gross income because the Tax Code excludes it. Examples include gain from a qualified sale of a principal residence, income earned abroad, and gifts and inheritances.

Exemption. A deduction for a taxpayer, spouse, and each dependent that is subtracted from income that would otherwise be taxed.

Fair market value. The amount at which property would change hands between a willing buyer and a willing seller, neither being under compulsion to buy or sell and both having reasonable knowledge of the relevant facts.

Filing status. One of five categories that a taxpayer is identified with. The five classifications are single, married filing jointly, married filing separately, head of household, and qualifying widow(er) with dependent child. It's important to choose the correct filing status, as it determines your standard deduction, the amount of tax you owe, and ultimately, any refund owed to you. If more than one filing status applies to you, choose the one that gives you the lowest tax obligation.

529 plan. Also known as a "Section 529 plan, a state-sponsored investment program under which a person can contribute to an account on behalf of a beneficiary for payment of qualified higher education expenses. The earnings in the account are allowed to grow tax-free, and there may be additional tax advantages upon distribution.

Forgiven debt. See Cancellation of debt

Investment income. Money earned on assets, like stock dividends, interest on bank accounts, etc.

Itemized deductions. Items, such as interest, state and local income and sales taxes, charitable contributions, and medical deductions, claimed on Schedule A of Form 1040. Itemized deductions are subtracted from adjusted gross income to arrive at taxable income. The amount of itemized deductions is also subject to a reduction when adjusted gross income exceeds certain limits. Taxpayers have the option of taking the "standard deduction" or itemizing their deductions.

Joint return. A return combining the income, exemptions, credits, and deductions of a married couple.

Taxpayers that file using this status are joint filers; they file jointly. See also Filing status

Kiddie tax. The tax on the investment income in excess of $1,900 of a child under age eighteen, based on the parents' marginal tax rate and computed on Form 8615.

Marginal rate. The tax bracket of the last dollar you earn for the year. For example, if you have $70,000 in taxable income, your marginal rate is 25 percent, so that if you earn another $100, your taxes would increase by $25.

Non-deductible. See Deduction

Phase out. The process by which certain tax benefits get reduced as a taxpayers' income increases.

PMI. Private mortgage insurance that protects lenders against default by borrowers. Most home buyers who can't afford a 20 percent down payment must buy PMI.

Primary residence or Principal residence. The primary location that a person inhabits. It doesn't matter whether it is a house, apartment, trailer, or boat, as long as it is where you live most of the time.

Refundable tax credit. A credit for which the IRS will send the taxpayer a refund for any amount in excess of the taxpayer's tax liability.

Refund anticipation loan. A loan provided by a third party against a taxpayer's expected refund. The tax refund anticipation loan is not

provided by the US Treasury or the IRS and is subject to the interest and fees set by the lender. These loans are most often offered by large tax preparation companies to taxpayers expecting refunds of a few thousands dollars or less.

Required minimum distribution (RMD). The amount that traditional, SEP-, and SIMPLE IRA owners and qualified plan participants must begin distributing from their retirement accounts by April 1 following the year they reach age 70.5. RMD amounts must then be distributed each subsequent year.

SEP-IRA. A retirement plan that an employer or self-employed individuals can establish. The employer is allowed a tax deduction for contributions made to the SEP plan and makes contributions to each eligible employee's SEP IRA on a discretionary basis.

Shifting income. The process of implementing a strategy that allows a transfer of income from one person to another person, presumably in a lower tax bracket.

Single. The filing status used by an unmarried taxpayer who does not qualify for any other filing status.

Standard deduction. An amount provided by the tax law in lieu of itemized deductions. A taxpayer whose gross income is not more than the sum of the standard deduction and exemptions generally does not have to pay tax. The amount varies according to filing status. An additional amount is allowed for taxpayers 65 or older or blind. Taxpayers who may be claimed as dependents on other taxpayers' returns may have a reduced standard deduction.

Stepped-up basis. The readjustment of the value of an appreciated asset for tax purposes upon inheritance. Usually, when an asset is passed on to a beneficiary, its value has increased from when the original owner acquired it.

Tax bracket. The rate at which income at a particular level is taxed.

Tax credit. A tax credit directly reduces tax liability, as opposed to a deduction that reduces income subject to tax.

Tax evasion. An illegal practice where someone intentionally avoids paying his or her taxes. Those caught evading taxes are generally subject to criminal charges and substantial penalties.

Taxable income. Taxable income is your adjusted gross income, minus your itemized deductions (or the standard deduction) and your exemptions.

UGMA and UTMA (Uniform Gifts to Minors Act and Uniform Transfers to Minors Act). Government acts that authorize minors to own property or other securities. The IRS allows persons to give so many thousands of dollars to another person without any tax consequences. If this recipient person is a minor, the UGMA permits the minor to own the assets without a lawyer setting up a trust fund. Under the UGMA, the ownership of the funds works like it does with any other trust, except that the donor must appoint a custodian (the trustee) to look after the account.

Unearned income. Taxable income other than that received for services performed (earned income). Unearned income includes money received for the investment of money or other property, such as interest, dividends, and royalties. It also includes pensions, alimony, unemployment compensation, and other income that is not earned.

Unreimbursed expense. Money spent by a taxpayer that was not repaid by their employer.

INDEX

NOTES

Do you have a great hint or tip to help save money or time? Share it with us! If we feature it in our next revision of Who Knew? or our next book, we'll be sure to include your name next to the hint.

Just email us at **hintsandtips@castlepointpub. com**, and please include your contact information so we can reach you if we decide to include your submission.

To reach us by mail, just send your hint to:
Hints and Tips
Castle Point Publishing
PO Box 1090
Hoboken, NJ 07030

Don't forget to include your return address or email address.

And thanks for your help!